The Joy of Christmas

The Joy
of
Christmas

ACCESS PUBLISHING

Available from
Church Resource Distributors
Phone (417) 831-7000

$\mathcal{C}$ONTENTS

$\mathscr{I}$NTRODUCTION

$\mathscr{T}$he life of Jesus Christ is the turning point of all history. Our calendar is hinged on His birth. Who was this man from the small town of Nazareth in the Middle East? Hundreds of years before He came, prophets announced His coming. Many great men have appeared in this world, yet none were divine and announced beforehand, except this one man— Jesus.

Almost 2,000 years ago, four writers recorded the life and teachings of Jesus. The first four books in the New Testament bear their names: Matthew, Mark, Luke and John.

Mark's record is the earliest of the four accounts. He was only a boy during Jesus' ministry on earth, but he later traveled with the apostle Peter. Mark wrote what Peter preached about Jesus.

Matthew, like Peter, was one of Jesus' twelve disciples. He offers a first-hand account of what Jesus said and did. Matthew wrote his life of Christ while giving pastoral leadership to the great missionary church in Antioch.

Luke was a physician who became a follower of Jesus after His life on earth. He spent time with many who were close to Jesus during His earthly ministry. Jesus' mother, Mary, gave Luke a mother's insight into Jesus' birth and early life.

The apostle John was the disciple who stood alone at the foot of the cross. When Jesus died, He demonstrated His great trust in John by committing the care of His mother, Mary, to him. At the time he wrote the last of the four histories, John was the only disciple still living.

In these readings about Jesus, you will see how detailed prophecies concerning His coming perfectly fit the four accounts of His life on earth. The Old Testament prophecies concerning Jesus are from the King James Version of the Bible and are in **bold-faced type**. Words of introduction and explanation that are not part of the Bible text are in *italics*. All of the Bible passages used are listed at the bottom of the last page of each daily reading.

When you read through Christ's life you will discover why the Bible is the best selling book of all time. You will not only learn who Jesus is, you will also discover why you were born. As you learn about His life, you will find that He touches the very center of your life.

$\mathcal{C}$HAPTER 1

Most people think of the Christmas story beginning in a manger in the little town of Bethlehem. The story really began before this world was created.

$\mathcal{T}$*he apostle John wrote,* In the beginning was the Word, and the Word was with God, and the Word was God. The Word became a man and lived among us, and we saw His glory. This glory belonged to the only Son, who came from the Father, and who was full of grace and truth.

We are told in the book of Hebrews, A long time ago, God spoke to the fathers through the prophets many times and in different ways. He has spoken to us in these last days through His Son, whom He chose as heir to all things. God also made the world through Him. The Son shows the glory of God. He is the exact image of God's nature, and keeps all things together by His powerful word.

The Bible tells us, There was a priest named Zechariah, during the time Herod was king of Judea. Zechariah was in the group of priests named

Abijah. He had a wife named Elizabeth who was one of the daughters of Aaron. They were both righteous in the sight of God and they obeyed completely the commands and orders of the Lord. They did not have any children because Elizabeth could not give birth to a child, and they were both very old.

During the time that Zechariah was doing his work as a priest in the presence of God, when his group was on duty in the temple, an angel from the Lord appeared to Zechariah. He stood at the right-hand side of the altar where the incense was burned. Zechariah was troubled when he saw the angel, and he became full of fear.

But the angel said to him, "Zechariah, don't be afraid, because your prayer has been heard. Your wife will give birth to a son for you and you will name him John, and he will cause many of the people of Israel to turn to the Lord their God."

Then Zechariah said to the angel, "How can I be sure of this? I am an old man and my wife is also old."

The angel answered him, "I am Gabriel, who stands in the presence of God. I was sent to speak to you and to bring this good news to you. Listen carefully; you will not be able to speak until the day when these things happen. This is because you did not believe my words that will become true at the right time."

The people waited for Zechariah, and they were surprised because he was in the temple for a long time. He could not speak to them when he came out, and they knew he had seen a vision. Zechariah made signs to them, but he still couldn't speak.

His wife, Elizabeth, became pregnant after this happened. She hid herself for five months.

The angel Gabriel was sent from God in the sixth month to a city named Nazareth, in Galilee. He was sent to a virgin whose name was Mary. She was going to be married to a man named Joseph, who was from the house of David.

More than 700 years before, the Holy Spirit inspired the Jewish prophet Isaiah to say, **Therefore the Lord himself shall give you a sign; Behold, a virgin shall conceive, and bear a son, and shall call his name Immanuel.**

The angel came to Mary and said, "Greetings to you who are favored very much. The Lord is with you."

But she was very troubled because of what he said, and thought about what kind of greeting this was.

Then the angel said to her, "Mary, don't be

afraid, because you are favored by God. You will conceive in your body and give birth to a son, and you will name Him Jesus. He will be great and will be called the Son of the Most High God. The Lord God will give Him the throne of His father David. He will rule over the house of Jacob forever, and His kingdom will never end."

Then Mary said to the angel, "How can this happen, because I am a virgin?"

The angel answered her, "The Holy Spirit will come to you, and the power of the Most High God will be over you. So the Holy One who is born will be named the Son of God. Elizabeth, a member of your family, has also conceived a son during her old age. She has never had a child, but now she has had a baby inside her body for six months. All things are possible for God to do."

Then Mary said, "I am a servant of the Lord. Let it happen to me as you have said."

The angel left her after this.

At that time Mary got up and went quickly to a town that was in the hills of Judah. She went into the house of Zechariah and greeted Elizabeth. The baby jumped in Elizabeth's body when she heard Mary's greeting.

Elizabeth was filled with the Holy Spirit and said in a loud voice, "You are blessed among women and the child in your body is blessed. Why do I receive this special favor, that the mother of my Lord comes to me? The baby in my body jumped because of joy when I heard your voice greeting me. This woman who believed is blessed because the things that the Lord has spoken to her will become true."

Then Mary said, "My soul praises the Lord, and my spirit is full of joy because of God, my Savior. He has seen and cared about His servant's humble kind of life. People in all generations will say I am blessed, now and forever."

Mary stayed with Elizabeth for about three months, and then she returned home.

The time came for Elizabeth to have her baby, and she gave birth to a son.

They came to circumcise the child on the eighth day after he was born, and they wanted to name him Zechariah, like his father, but his mother answered, "No, he will be named John."

So they made signs to the baby's father to see what he wanted the son's name to be.

He asked for a piece of paper and wrote, "His name is John."

Zechariah's tongue was made free, and he began to speak and praise the Lord. The child grew, and his spirit became strong; and he was in the wilderness until the day when he let the people in Israel see him.

Now the birth of Jesus Christ happened this way. Mary, His mother, was promised to be married to Joseph.

It was found that the Holy Spirit caused Mary to have a child inside her before she and Joseph were married.

Joseph, her husband, was a righteous man and he did not want to shame her publicly. So he decided to divorce her secretly. But an angel from the Lord appeared to him in a dream, while he thought about these things.

The angel said to him, "Joseph, you who are from the family of David, do not be afraid to take Mary to be your wife, because the baby who is inside her is from the Holy Spirit. She will give birth to a son, and you will name Him 'Jesus,' because He will save His people from their sins."

All these things happened so what the Lord spoke through the prophet Isaiah could become true. Isaiah said, **"Behold, a virgin shall conceive,** and bear a son, and shall call his name Immanuel, which being interpreted is God with us."

Then Joseph woke from his sleep and did what the angel from the Lord ordered him to do. He took Mary to be his wife.

During those days Caesar Augustus ordered that all the names of the people in the world were to be recorded. So everyone went to their own city to have their names recorded.

Joseph also went from the city of Nazareth in Galilee to the city of Bethlehem in Judea. Bethlehem is named the city of David.

Joseph went there because he was from the house and the family of David. He went there to record himself and Mary, who was going to marry him.

This fulfilled a prophecy made by God's Spirit through the Jewish prophet Micah 700 years before, when Micah said, **But thou, Bethlehem Ephrathah, though thou be little among the thousands of Judah, yet out of thee shall he come forth unto me that is to be ruler in Israel.**

Mary already had a child inside her, and the time came for her to give birth when they were still in Bethlehem.

Then she gave birth to her first son, and she

wrapped a long cloth around Him. She put Him in a manger because there was not any room for them at the inn.

There were some shepherds who were staying in the fields near there, guarding their sheep during the night. An angel from the Lord suddenly was with them. The glory of the Lord shined on them, and they were full of fear.

But the angel said to them, "Do not be afraid, because I bring you good news about great joy for all people. Your Savior was born today in the city of David. He is Christ the Lord. You will know you have found Him when you see a baby in a manger with a long cloth around Him."

Suddenly, a large number of the angels from heaven were with this angel, and they praised God and said, "Glory to God in the highest heavens and peace be on earth among men with whom God is pleased."

The shepherds said to each other after the angels went away, "Let's go to Bethlehem and see this thing that the Lord told us has happened."

They came quickly and found Mary and Joseph, and the baby who was in the manger.

Then the shepherds returned and praised God.

They gave Him glory for all the things they heard and saw, because everything happened just as they had been told.

The time came to circumcise the baby after eight days, and He was named Jesus, because the angel had given Him this name before Jesus was formed in Mary's body.

The law of Moses taught that they had to be made pure, and they brought Jesus to Jerusalem to present Him to the Lord when that time ended. It is written in the law of the Lord, "Every male who is the child born first in a family will be given to the Lord for His service." The law of the Lord taught that they must offer a sacrifice of two doves or two young pigeons.

There was a man named Simeon in Jerusalem, who was righteous and holy. He was waiting for comfort and help from God for Israel, and he was filled with the Holy Spirit. The Holy Spirit told him that he would not die before he saw the Lord's Christ. The Spirit led Simeon into the temple.

The parents brought in the little child, Jesus, to do what the law of tradition taught.

Simeon took Jesus in his arms and blessed God. He said, "Now Lord, You are letting your servant leave in peace, just as you promised, because my eyes have seen Your Salvation that you have made ready for all people to see. He will be a light for revelation to the Gentiles, and praise and glory to your people Israel."

Simeon was confirming the arrival of the Messiah, prophesied by Isaiah hundreds of years before, **Arise, shine; for thy light is come, and the glory of the Lord is risen upon thee. And the Gentiles shall come to thy light, and kings to the brightness of thy rising.**

Jesus' father and mother were very surprised because of the things that were said about Him.

Then Simeon blessed them and said to Mary, his mother, "This child will cause many people to be destroyed and many to be saved in Israel. He will be a sign that people speak against. A sword will even go through your own soul. And thoughts in many hearts will be shown."

Wise men from the East came to Jerusalem.

They said, "Where is the Child Who was born and is King of the Jews? We saw His star in the East, and we came to worship Him."

Herod the King and all the other people in Jerusalem were troubled when they heard this.

Herod asked all the chief priests and teachers of

the people to come together, and he asked where the Christ would be born.

They said to him, "He will be born in Bethlehem in Judea, because it is written by God's prophet, Micah, 'And thou Bethlehem, in the land of Judah, art not the least among the princes of Judah: for out of thee shall come a Governor, that shall rule my people Israel.'"

Then Herod asked the wise men to come secretly, and he learned from them the exact time the star appeared.

Then he sent them to Bethlehem and said, "Go and search carefully for the young child. Tell me when you find Him, so I can also go and worship Him."

They left after they heard what the king said.

The star they saw in the East went in front of them and stopped above the place where the young child was.

They spoke with very great joy when they saw the star.

The wise men came into the house and saw the young child with Mary, His mother, and they went down on their knees and worshiped Him.

They opened their bags that were filled with

expensive things, and they gave gifts of gold, frankincense, and myrrh to Him. God warned them in a dream not to return to Herod, so they went back to their country another way.

Again the words of the Spirit of God through Isaiah had been fulfilled, **They shall bring gold and incense; and they shall show forth the praises of the Lord.**

John 1:1,14; Hebrews 1:1-3; Luke 1:5-8; Luke 1:11-13; Luke 1:16; Luke 1:18-22; Luke 1:24; Luke 1:26-27; Isaiah 7:14; Luke 1:28-48; Luke 1:56-57; Luke 1:59-60; Luke 1:62-64; Luke 1:80; Matthew 1:18-24; Luke 2:1; Luke 2:3-5; Micah 5:2; Luke 2:5-16; Luke 2:20; Luke 2:21-32; Isaiah 60:1,3; Luke 2:33-34; Matthew 2:1-2; Matthew 2:3-12; Micah 5:2; Isaiah 60:6

CHAPTER 2

An angel from the Lord appeared to Joseph in a dream after the wise men went away, and he said, "Get up, take the child and His mother, and go to Egypt. Stay there until I tell you to leave, because Herod will look for the child so he can kill Him."

Joseph got up and took the young child and His mother during the night, and went to Egypt. They stayed there until Herod died, so what the Lord spoke through the prophet Hosea could become true, **"Out of Egypt have I called my son."**

Herod was very angry when he knew the wise men had tricked him. He ordered his men to kill all the male children in Bethlehem and in the places near it, who were two years old and younger, because this was the exact time that he had learned from the wise men.

An angel from the Lord appeared in a dream to Joseph in Egypt, after Herod died. He said, "Get up. Take the young child and His mother, and go to the country of Israel, because the people who tried to kill the child are dead."

Joseph got up and took the young child and his mother, and went into Israel.

More than 750 years before this happened, the Jewish prophet Hosea said, **When Israel was a child, then I loved him, and called my son out of Egypt.**

But Joseph was afraid to go to Judea when he heard that Archelaus was the ruler there instead of his father, Herod.

God warned Joseph in a dream, so he went away to the area of Galilee to live in a city named Nazareth. Thus, what was spoken through the prophets, that He would be called a Nazarene, could become true.

The child grew and became strong. He was full of wisdom, and the grace of God was with Him.

Jesus' parents went to Jerusalem every year for the Passover Feast.

They went to the Feast when Jesus was twelve years old, because their tradition taught this.

The days of the Feast ended, and the child Jesus stayed in Jerusalem while all the other people returned home. His parents did not know about this because they thought He was with the people in their group.

They traveled for a day, and then they searched for Him among their family and friends. When they did not find Him, they returned to Jerusalem to search for Him.

They found Him in the temple after three days. He was sitting with the teachers.

He listened to the teachers and asked them questions, and everyone who heard Him was very surprised because He understood and answered very well.

His parents were very surprised when they saw Him, and His mother said to Him, "Son, why did You do this to us? Your father and I have searched for You, and we were very worried."

Then He said to them, "Why did you search for Me? Don't you know I must do the kinds of things that My Father wants?"

They did not understand what He said to them.

He went with them to Nazareth, and He obeyed whatever they told Him to do. But His mother kept in her heart all the things that were said.

Jesus increased in wisdom and in age, and in favor with God and people.

More than 700 years before, the Jewish prophet Isaiah foretold, **The voice of him that crieth in the** wilderness, **Prepare ye the way of the Lord, make straight in the desert a highway for our God.**

John the Baptizer came at that time. He preached in the wilderness of Judea.

He said, "Repent, because the kingdom of heaven is near."

John wore clothes made from camel's hair, and a leather belt around his waist. His food was locusts and wild honey.

People came to him from Jerusalem, Judea, and from all the places near the Jordan River. He baptized them in the Jordan River, when they admitted their sins.

Then Jesus came from Nazareth in Galilee, and John baptized Him in the Jordan River.

Jesus came up from the water immediately, and He saw the sky open and the Spirit of God come down on Him like a dove.

A voice from the sky said, "You are my dear Son. I love You, and You have pleased me very much."

This had been foretold by the prophet Isaiah, **And the Spirit of the Lord shall rest upon him,** *and by King David,* **The Lord hath said unto me, "Thou art my Son..."**

Then the Spirit led Jesus into the wilderness to

be tested by Satan. He did not eat anything for 40 days and 40 nights, and He was hungry.

The one who tested Him came and said to Him, "Order these stones to become loaves of bread, if you are the Son of God."

But Jesus answered, "It is written, 'People will not live by bread only, but they will live by every word that comes from the mouth of God.'"

Then Satan took Him into Jerusalem and put Him on the highest place of the temple.

Satan said to Him, "Throw yourself down if you are the Son of God, because it is written, 'God will give orders about you to His angels and the angels will lift you up with their hands, so you will not hit your foot against a stone.'"

Jesus said to him, "Again it is written, 'Do not test the Lord your God.'"

But the Devil took Him again to a very high mountain and showed Him all the kingdoms of the world and their greatness.

He said to Him, "I will give you all these things if you will go down on your knees and worship me."

Then Jesus said to him, "Satan, go away from me, because it is written, 'Worship the Lord your God, and serve Him only.'"

Then Satan went away from Him, and the angels came and helped Him.

This is what John said, when the Jews sent priests and Levites to him from Jerusalem to ask him who he was. He did not lie.

He told the truth, "I am not the Christ."

They asked him, "So who are you? Are you Elijah?"

He said, "I am not."

They asked, "Are you the Prophet?"

He answered, "No."

So they said to him, "Who are you? Tell us so we can give an answer to the people who sent us. What do you say about yourself?"

He said, "I am the voice of a man who calls out in the wilderness, 'Make the Lord's road straight,' just as Isaiah the prophet said."

The people who were sent from the Pharisees asked him, "So why do you baptize people, if you are not the Christ, or Elijah, or the Prophet?"

John answered them, "I baptize people with water, but there is someone among you whom you do not know. He is the One who will come later. I am not good enough to even untie His shoe."

All these things happened in Bethany, across the

Jordan river, where John baptized people.

John saw Jesus coming toward him the next day, and he said, "Look, here is the Lamb of God who takes away the sins of the world! This is the man I was talking about when I said, 'A man who is greater than I am will come later. He is greater because He existed before I was born.' I did not know Him, but I came and baptized people with water, so He could be made known to Israel."

John told them what he had seen.

He said, "I saw the Spirit come down from heaven like a dove, and it remained on Him. I did not know Him, but the One who sent me to baptize people with water said to me, 'The person on whom you see the Spirit come down and remain, He is the One who will baptize people with the Holy Spirit.' I saw this, and I tell you that He is the Son of God."

John was there again with two of his followers the next day.

He saw Jesus walking there, and he said, "Look, here is the Lamb of God!" His two followers heard him say this, and they followed Jesus.

Jesus turned and saw them following Him and said to them, "What do you want?"

They said to Him, "Rabbi (that means 'teacher'),

where do you live?"

He said to them, "Come, and you will see."

So they went and saw the place where He lived, and they stayed there with Him that day. It was four o'clock in the afternoon.

Andrew, Simon Peter's brother, was one of the two men who heard John speak about Jesus and who had followed Him.

He found his brother Simon first, and said to him, "We have found the Messiah (that means 'The Christ.')."

He brought Peter to Jesus, and Jesus looked at him and said, "You are Simon, the son of John. You will be called Cephas (that means, 'Peter')."

Jesus decided to go to Galilee the next day, and He found Philip and said to him, "Follow me."

Philip was from Bethsaida, the city from which Andrew and Peter had come.

Philip found Nathanael and said to him, "We have found the man whom Moses wrote about in the law and whom the prophets also wrote about. He is Joseph's son, Jesus from Nazareth."

Nathanael said to him, "Can anything good come from Nazareth?"

Philip said to him, "Come and see."

Jesus saw Nathanael coming toward Him, and He said to him, "Look, here is a real Israelite. There is nothing false in him!"

Nathanael said to Him, "How do you know me?"

Jesus answered him, "I saw you when you were sitting under the fruit tree, even before Philip told you to come."

Nathanael answered Him, "Teacher, you are the Son of God. You are the King of Israel."

Jesus answered Nathanael, "You believe in me because I told you I saw you under the fruit tree? You will see greater things than these."

He said to him, "I tell you the truth, you will see heaven open, and you will see the angels of God going up and coming down on the Son of Man."

There was a marriage at Cana in Galilee on the third day, and Jesus' mother was there.

Jesus and His followers were also invited to the marriage.

Jesus' mother said to Him, after there was no more wine, "They do not have any more wine."

There were six stone water pots there. The Jews used them to wash themselves in the religious way to make themselves pure. Each of these pots could hold twenty or thirty gallons of water.

Jesus said to them, "Fill the pots with water," and they filled them up to the top.

He said to them, "Take some of the water out now, and take it to the master of the feast."

They did this, and the master tasted the water that had now become wine. He did not know where the wine came from, but the servants who had taken the water knew where it came from.

The master of the feast called the bridegroom to him and said, "Everyone always gives the good wine to people first, and then gives the wine that is not as good to the guests after they have drunk too much. But you have kept the good wine until now."

This was the beginning of the miracles Jesus did at Cana in Galilee, and He made known His greatness and power, and His followers believed in Him.

Matthew 2:13-21; Hosea 11:1; Hosea 11:1; Matthew 2:22,23; Luke 2:40-52; Isaiah 40:3; Matthew 3:1-2; Matthew 3:4-6; Mark 1:9-11; Matthew 4:1-11; John 1:19-34; John 1:35-49; Isaiah 11:2; John 1:50-2:3; John 2:6-11

CHAPTER 3

One of the Pharisees, named Nicodemus, was a ruler of the Jews.

He came to Jesus during the night and said to Him, "Rabbi, we know You are a teacher who came from God, because no one can do these miracles that You do unless God is with Him."

Jesus answered him, "I tell you the truth, a person cannot see the kingdom of God unless he is born again."

Nicodemus said to Him, "How can a man be born again when he is old? Can he go into his mother's body a second time to be born again?"

Jesus answered, "I tell you the truth, a person cannot go into the kingdom of God unless he is born from water and from the Spirit. A body gives birth to a body, but the Spirit gives birth to the spirit. Do not be surprised when I tell you, 'You must be born again.'

"God loved the world so much that He gave His only Son, so any person who believes in Him will not die, but will have everlasting life. God did not send His Son into the world to condemn the world, but to save the world through Him.

"Any person who believes in Him is not condemned, but any person who does not believe is condemned already, because that person has not believed in the name of God's only Son.

"The light has come into the world, but people loved the darkness rather than the light because the things they did were evil. Any person who does evil things hates the light. That person does not come to the light, so the things he does will not be seen.

"But any person who does the things that are true comes to the light, so people can see that what he has done has been done through God."

And so He came to a city in Samaria named Sychar, which is near the piece of ground Jacob gave to his son, Joseph.

Jacob's well was there, so Jesus sat down near the well, because He was tired after the trip. It was about three o'clock in the afternoon then. A woman from Samaria came to get some water, and Jesus said to her, "Give me a drink."

The Samaritan woman said to Him, "Why do You ask me for a drink, since You are a Jew, and I am a Samaritan woman?" (This was because Jews were not friendly to Samaritans.)

Jesus answered her, "Everyone who drinks this water will be thirsty again, but anyone who drinks the water I give him will never be thirsty again. The water I give him will become a spring of water in him that will rise up and give everlasting life."

The woman said to Him, "Sir, give me this water, so I will not be thirsty again or have to come here to get water."

Jesus said to her, "Go and call your husband, and then come here again."

The woman answered Him, "I do not have a husband."

Jesus said to her, "You are right when you say you do not have a husband, because you had five husbands, and the man you have now is not your husband. What you just said is true."

The woman said to Him, "Sir, I can see that You are a prophet."

Many Samaritans from that city believed in Jesus because of the things the woman told them.

She said, "He told me everything I ever did."

So the Samaritans asked Jesus to stay with them when they came to Him, and He stayed there for two days. Many other people believed in Him because of His message.

They said to the woman, "We believe now not because of what you said, but because we have heard these things ourselves. We know this man really is the Savior of the world."

Jesus went to Nazareth, where He lived when He was a child, and He went into the synagogue on the sabbath day like He always did.

Then He stood to read, and the book of the prophet Isaiah was given to Him.

He opened the book and found the place where it is written, **"The Spirit of the Lord is upon me; because He hath anointed me to preach the gospel to the poor; he hath sent me to heal the broken-hearted, to preach deliverance to the captives, and recovering of sight to the blind, to set at liberty them that are bruised, to preach the acceptable year of the Lord."**

Then He closed the book and gave it to the helper and sat down.

Everyone in the synagogue looked at Jesus, and He said to them, "What God said in these words a long time ago has happened in your presence today."

All of them agreed with what He said and they were surprised because of the wonderful words that came out of His mouth.

They said, "Isn't this Joseph's son?"

Then Jesus said to them, "I am sure you will say to me, 'Doctor, heal yourself, and do here in your home town the same things that we heard that you did at Capernaum.'"

He continued, "I tell you the truth, a prophet is not accepted in his home town. I tell you, there were many widows in Israel during the time of Elijah when there was no rain for three and a half years. There was not any food in all of the country, but Elijah was not sent to any of these people. He was sent to a widow in Zarephath, near Sidon. Also, there were many lepers in Israel during the time of the prophet, Elisha, but none of the lepers were made clean except Naaman who was from Syria."

All of the people in the synagogue were full of anger when they heard these things.

They stood, ordered Him to leave the city, and brought Him to the edge of the hill on which their city was built so they could throw Him down the hill.

But He walked through the crowd of people and left.

Jesus saw Simon and his brother, Andrew, throw a fishing net into the Sea of Galilee as He walked near them. They were fishermen.

Jesus said to them, "Come and follow me, and I

will change you into men who fish for people."

They went away from their nets immediately and followed Him.

Jesus saw James, the son of Zebedee, and his brother John, as He walked a little farther. They were also in the boat making their nets ready for fishing.

Jesus called them immediately, and they went away from their father, who was in the boat with the workers, and they followed Jesus.

Jesus saw the mother of Peter's wife lying sick with a fever when He came into Peter's house. He touched her hand and the fever left. Then she got up and served Him.

They brought many people who were controlled by evil spirits to Jesus, when it was evening.

He ordered the spirits to leave by saying only a word, and He healed everyone who was sick.

So what Isaiah the prophet spoke became true, **"Himself took our infirmities, and bare our sicknesses."**

Jesus went in a boat to the other side of the lake to His own city.

Then some men carried a man on a sleeping mat, who could not move his body.

They tried to bring him into the house to lay him

in front of Jesus. They could not find a way to bring him in because of the crowd of people.

Then they went up to the roof of the house and brought him down on his sleeping mat through a hole in the roof. They put him in the middle of the crowd in front of Jesus.

He saw their faith and said, "Friend, your sins are forgiven."

Some of the teachers of the Law said to themselves, "This Man does not have any respect for God and He says evil things."

Jesus knew their thoughts and said, "Why do you think evil thoughts in your hearts? Is it easier to say, 'Your sins are forgiven,' or to say, 'Stand and walk'? But this is so you will know that the Son of Man has authority on earth to forgive sins."

Then Jesus said to the man who could not move his body, "Stand, take your sleeping mat, and go to your house."

He stood and went to his house.

But the people in the crowds were afraid when they saw it, and they thanked and praised God for giving this kind of authority to men.

These miracles of Jesus had been foretold seven hundred years earlier, when the Spirit of God said through

Isaiah, **Then the eyes of the blind shall be opened, and the ears of the deaf shall be unstopped. Then shall the lame man leap as a deer, and the tongue of the dumb sing.**

Jesus went out after that, and He saw a man named Levi who collected taxes.

He was at the place where people came to pay their taxes, and Jesus said, "Follow Me."

And he left everything and stood and followed Him.

Levi made a very large feast for Jesus at his house. There also was eating there with them a large crowd of men who collected taxes, and other people.

The Pharisees and their teachers of the Law complained to the followers of Jesus and said, "Why do you eat and drink with people who are sinners and with men who collect taxes?"

Jesus answered them, "People who are healthy do not need a doctor; only people who are sick need one. I did not come to ask the people who are righteous to follow Me. I came to ask the people who are sinners to repent."

Jesus walked through the grain fields on a Sabbath Day. His followers took some grain, rubbed it in their hands, and ate it.

But some of the Pharisees said, "Why do you do something on the Sabbath that is against the Law?"

Jesus answered them, "Didn't you read what David did when he and the men with him were hungry? David went into God's house and took the bread that was offered to God and ate it. He also gave it to the men who were with him. This is against the Law, because only priests are allowed to eat this bread."

Jesus said to them, "The Sabbath was made for man. Man was not made for the Sabbath. So the Son of Man has authority over even the Sabbath."

Jesus went into a synagogue again. A man with a crippled hand was there. The people watched to see if Jesus would heal him on the Sabbath Day, so they could say evil things against Him.

Jesus said to the man with the crippled hand, "Stand and come in front of everyone."

He said to the people, "Is it right to do good things on the Sabbath Day, or to do evil things? Is it right to save a life, or to kill someone?"

They remained quiet. He looked at all of them with anger, and He was deeply sad because their hearts were hard.

Then Jesus said to the man, "Reach out your hand."

He reached out his hand, and it was healed completely.

The Pharisees went out and began to plan immediately with the Herodians to kill Jesus.

Then Jesus went up to the mountain and He called the men He wanted to come to Him, and they came to Him. He chose twelve of them to be with Him and to go out to preach and to have authority to order the evil spirits to leave.

Jesus went up to the mountains when He saw the crowds, and the twelve followers came to Him after He sat down. Then He opened His mouth and taught them.

He said, "People who are poor in spirit are blessed, because the kingdom of heaven belongs to them.

"People who are deeply sad are blessed, because they will be comforted.

"People who are gentle are blessed, because they will inherit the earth.

"People who are hungry and thirsty for righteousness are blessed, because they will be filled.

"People who are merciful to other people are blessed, because they will receive mercy.

"People who have pure hearts are blessed,

because they will see God.

"People who cause peace to come are blessed, because they will be called the sons of God.

"People who have been attacked and troubled because of righteousness are blessed, because the kingdom of heaven belongs to them. You are blessed when men speak against you, attack you, and say all kinds of evil things that are false against you because of Me. Have great joy and be happy because your reward in heaven is great, for in the same way, people attacked and troubled the prophets who were before you.

"Pray in this way, 'Our Father Who is in heaven, let Your name be greatly honored. Let Your kingdom come, and let what You want be done on earth, just as it is done in heaven. Give our daily food to us today, and forgive us for our sins, just as we also have forgiven people who sinned against us. Do not lead us into temptation, but save us from the evil one.'

"Your Father in heaven will forgive you, if you forgive people for their sins. But your Father will not forgive you for your sins if you do not forgive people."

Jesus began to teach near the sea again, and the crowd of people that came was very large. So He went into a boat and sat in it on the sea. All the crowd was on the land near the sea. He taught them many things in stories.

Jesus said to them in His teaching, "Listen carefully. A farmer went out to plant seeds. Some seeds fell at the side of the road when he planted them, and the birds came and ate them.

"Other seeds fell on ground that had many rocks and not much dirt. The plants came up immediately because the dirt was not deep. But the sun dried the plants quickly, and they died because they did not have any roots.

"Other seeds fell where there were many thorns. The thorns grew up and did not give the seeds enough space to grow, so they did not produce any grain.

"Other seeds fell on good ground, and they grew up and became large, and they produced 30, 60, and 100 times as much grain."

Jesus said, "You should listen if you have ears to hear with."

The Twelve and the other people following Him, who were near Jesus, asked Him about the stories when He was alone.

And Jesus said, "The story means that the seed is God's message.

"Those seeds at the side of the road are the people who hear God's message, but Satan comes and takes away the message from their hearts, so they cannot believe and be saved.

"Those seeds on the ground that had many rocks are the people who hear and receive the message with joy when they hear it. But they do not have any roots in them. They believe for a while, and they turn away from God when they have problems.

"Those seeds that fell where there were many thorns are the people who hear the message, but as they go on their way, the worries, riches, and pleasures of life don't give them enough room to grow, and they do not produce fruit that grows completely.

"The seeds in the good ground are the people who hear the message with honest and good hearts. They keep the message in their hearts and continue to produce fruit patiently."

John 3:1–7; John 3:16–21; John 4:5–7,9; John 4:13–19;
John 4:39–42; Luke 4:16–30; Mark 1:16–20; Matthew 8:14–17;
Isaiah 53:4; Matthew 9:1; Luke 5:18–20; Matthew 9:3–8;
Isaiah 35:5–6; Luke 5:27–32; Luke 6:1–4; Mark 2:27–3:6;
Mark 3:13–15; Matthew 5:1–12; Matthew 6:9–15; Mark 4:1–2;
Mark 4:3–10; Luke 8:11–15

CHAPTER 4

*J*esus spoke everything in stories to the crowds. He did not say anything to them without using a story.

"The kingdom of heaven is like a box of very valuable things that was hidden in the field. A man found it and hid it in the field again. He had great joy, and went and sold everything he owned, and bought that field.

"Again, the kingdom of God is like a businessman looking for valuable pearls. He found one pearl that was very valuable. So he went and sold everything he had and bought the pearl.

"Again, the kingdom of heaven is like a net that was thrown into the sea. It caught fish of every kind, and the men pulled the net to the shore after it was filled. Then they sat down and put the good fish into baskets, but they threw away the bad ones.

"So this is what will happen at the end of the world. The angels will come and separate the people who are evil from the people who are righteous. They will throw the evil ones into the place where the fire is, and there will be loud cries and sounds of great fear and anger."

Ten centuries earlier the use of stories in Jesus' teaching was also foretold in the Psalms, **I will open my mouth in a parable.**

It was evening on that day, and Jesus said to His followers, "Let's go over to the other side."

They went away from the crowd of people and took Jesus with them in the boat. There were also other boats with Him.

A very strong storm with much wind came, and the waves came into the boat, and the boat was filled with water.

Jesus was sleeping in the back of the boat on a cushion.

They woke Him and said to Him, "Teacher, don't You care if we die?"

He got up and ordered the wind to stop, and said to the waves of the sea, "Be quiet and stop!"

The wind stopped, and everything was completely calm.

He said to them, "Why are you full of fear? Do you still not have any faith?"

They were full of fear, and they said to each other, "Who is this? Even the wind and the sea obey Him!"

The psalmist foretold, **Thou rulest the raging of the sea; when the waves thereof arise, thou stillest them.**

A ruler came and worshiped Jesus. He said, "My daughter just died. But come and put Your hand on her, and she will live."

Jesus stood and followed him. His followers also went with Him.

There was a woman who had blood coming out from her body for twelve years. She came behind Jesus and touched the edge of His clothes, because she was saying to herself, "I will be healed if I can just touch His clothes."

Jesus turned and saw her, and said, "Daughter, have courage. Your faith has healed you."

The woman was healed immediately.

Jesus saw the men playing the flutes when He came into the ruler's house. He also saw the troubled and noisy crowd.

He said, "Go, because the girl is not dead but she is asleep."

They laughed at Him, but He went in after the crowd was sent out.

He took the girl's hand, and she was raised up. People told about this everywhere in all the places near there.

When the apostles returned, they told Jesus all the things they had done. Then Jesus took them alone with Him to a town called Bethsaida.

But the crowd of people knew this and followed Him. Jesus welcomed them and spoke to them about the kingdom of God, and He healed the people who needed to be healed.

But it was already late in the day, and the Twelve came and said to Him, "Send the crowd of people away, so they can go to the towns and to the farms near here to sleep and get food, because we are far away from other places here."

But Jesus said to the apostles, "Give them something to eat."

They said, "We have only five loaves of bread and two fish. We can feed all these people only if we go and buy food for them."

There were about 5,000 men.

Then Jesus said to His followers, "Tell the people to sit in groups of about 50 people in each group."

The apostles did this, and all of the people sat down.

Jesus took the five loaves of bread and two fish, and He looked up to heaven and blessed them.

Then He broke them into pieces. He gave the

food to His followers to give to the people in the crowd.

All of them ate and they had enough. And the apostles filled twelve baskets with the broken pieces that remained.

The people saw the miracle Jesus did and they said, "It is true that this is the Prophet Who is to come into the world."

Jesus knew that they were going to come soon and take Him by force to make Him King, so He went away again alone to the mountain.

He told His followers to go into the boat immediately and to go ahead of Him to the other side of the sea, while He sent the crowds away.

He went alone to the mountain to pray after He had sent the crowds away. He was there alone when it was evening.

But the boat was now far from the shore and was shaken strongly by the waves because the wind was coming against it.

Jesus walked on the sea and came toward His followers between three and six o'clock in the morning. They were troubled when they saw Him walking on the sea.

They said, "It is a spirit," and they cried out

because they were afraid.

Jesus spoke to them immediately and said, "Have courage and do not be afraid. It is I."

Peter answered Him and said, "Lord, ask me to come to You on the water if it is You."

Jesus said, "Come."

Then Peter went out from the boat and walked on the water toward Jesus.

But he was afraid when he saw the wind, and he cried out as he began to go down into the water, "Lord, save me!"

Jesus reached out His hand immediately and put His hand on Peter and held him.

He said to him, "You who don't have much faith, why did you doubt?"

The wind stopped when they went into the boat.

The men who were in the boat worshiped Jesus and said, "It is true that You are the Son of God."

From that time on, Jesus began to explain to His followers that He must go to Jerusalem, and the religious leaders, chief priests, and teachers of the Law must do many things to Him that would cause Him to suffer.

He told them that He must be killed and be brought back to life three days after He was killed.

Peter took Him away from the other people and rebuked Him, "Lord, let it never be! This will never happen to You."

But Jesus turned and said to Peter, "Satan, go away from me! You are trying to stop me because you do not have the thoughts of God in your mind, but you have the thoughts of men."

Hundreds of years before this, Isaiah had prophesied, **Yet it pleased the Lord to bruise him; he hath put him to grief. When thou shalt make his soul an offering for sin ....**

Then He said to all of them, "A person must give up his own desires and take up his cross every day and obey me, if he wants to follow me. A person will lose his life if he wants to save it, and a person will save his life if he loses it for me.

"What has a person gained if he has gained all of the world, but gives up himself for it? If anyone feels shame, because of Me and My words, the Son of Man will also feel shame because of that person when He comes in His glory and the glory of His Father and the holy angels."

Jesus took Peter, James, and John up to a high mountain.

Then Jesus became completely changed in front

of them. His clothes shone, and they were whiter than anyone in the world could make them.

Then Peter, James, and John saw Elijah and Moses, and they were talking with Jesus.

Then a cloud came over them, and a voice came out from the cloud, "This is my Son, whom I love. Listen to Him."

They looked and saw that suddenly no one was with them except Jesus.

As they came down from the mountain, Jesus ordered them not to tell anyone about the things they saw, until after the Son of Man would come back to life from death.

They did not tell anyone, and they asked each other questions about what Jesus said about coming back to life from death.

But the Pharisees came together when they heard that Jesus caused the Sadducees not to have any more to say.

One of them, who was an expert in the law, asked Him a question to test Him, "Teacher, which is the greatest command in the law?"

Jesus said to him, "'Love the Lord your God with all your heart, with all your soul, and with all your mind.' This is the first and greatest command. The second one is like it, 'Love your neighbor just like you love yourself.' All the Law and the Prophets depend on these two commands."

But the expert in the Law wanted to make himself right, and said to Jesus, "Who is my neighbor?"

Jesus answered, "A man went from Jerusalem to Jericho, and he met some thieves, who took his clothes and beat him. Then they went away and left him there half dead.

"Then a priest walked on that road, but he went on the other side of the road when he saw the man.

"In the same way, a Levite also came to that place and went by on the other side of the road when he saw the man.

"But a Samaritan who was travelling came to where the man was. He was full of mercy when he saw the man, and he came to him and put a cloth on his wounds. He also poured wine and oil on his wounds, put him on his donkey, and brought him to an inn and helped him.

"The next day, the Samaritan gave two denarii to the man who worked at the inn and said, 'Give him the things he needs, and if you spend more than these two denarii, I will pay you when I return again.'

"Which one of these three people is a neighbor

to the person who met the thieves?"

The expert in the law said, "The neighbor is the one who showed mercy to him."

Then Jesus said to him, "Go and do the same kinds of things."

All the sinners and the men who collected taxes came near Jesus to hear Him.

Both the Pharisees and the teachers of the Law complained and said, "This man welcomes sinners and eats with them."

Jesus told them this story, "If one of you has a hundred sheep and loses one of them, doesn't he leave the other ninety-nine sheep in the field and go after the one sheep that is lost until he finds it? He puts it on his back when he finds it and he has great joy. He calls his friends and neighbors when he comes home, and says to them, 'Be happy with me because I found my sheep that was lost.'

"I say to you, there will be more joy in heaven because of one sinner who repents than because of ninety-nine righteous people who do not need to repent."

Jesus said, "A man had two sons. The younger son said to his father, 'Father, give me the part of your riches that belongs to me.' So the father divided his riches between the two sons.

"A few days later, the younger son took all his things and went to a country far away. He wasted his money there by living the wrong kind of life.

"At that time, there was no longer any food in this country. He had spent all of his money, and he began to be hungry.

"He went and worked for a person from that country, and that person sent him into his fields to give food to the pigs. He wanted to eat the food that the pigs ate, but no one gave him anything to eat.

"When he admitted to himself that he had been foolish, he said, 'Many servants who work for my father have more than enough bread to eat, and I am dying from hunger here.' I will go to my father and say to him, 'Father, I have sinned against heaven and against you. I am not good enough to be called your son any longer. Let me be like one of your servants.'

"So he left and went to his father.

"But his father saw him when he was still far away, and his father was filled with love and mercy. He ran and put his arms around his son's neck and kissed him.

"The son said to him, 'Father, I have sinned against heaven and against you. I am not good enough to be called your son any longer.'

"But the father said to his servants, 'Bring out the best clothes quickly and put them on him, and put a ring on his hand and shoes on his feet. Bring the fat young cow and kill it, and let's eat and be happy, because this son was dead and is alive again. He was lost, but he is found now.'

"So they began to have a feast.

"This man's older son was in the field and he heard music and dancing as he came near to the house. He called one of the servants to him and asked him what was happening.

"The servant said to him, 'Your brother has returned, and your father killed the fat young cow because he has come back and he is safe and well.'

"The older son became angry and did not want to go in, and his father came out and begged him to go in.

"But he answered his father, 'I have helped you for many years and I always did what you told me to do. But you never killed a young goat for me, so I could have a feast with my friends. But when this son who wasted your money on prostitutes came home again, you killed the fat young cow for him.'

"His father said to him, 'Son, you have always

been here with me and everything that is mine belongs to you. But it was right to have a feast and be happy because your brother was dead, but he is alive again. He was lost, but he is found now.'"

Matthew 13:34; Matthew 13:44-50; Psalm 78:2; Mark 4:35-41;
Psalm 89:9; Matthew 9:18-26; Luke 9:10-17; John 6:14-15;
Matthew 14:22-33; Matthew 16:21-23; Isaiah 53:10;
Luke 9:23-26; Mark 9:2-4; Mark 9:7-10; Matthew 22:34;
Matthew 22:35-40; Luke 10:29-37; Luke 15:1-7; Luke 15:11-32

CHAPTER 5

*J*esus said, "There was a rich man who dressed in purple and fine clothes. His life was filled with riches and pleasure every day.

"Some people put a poor man named Lazarus at the rich man's gate. His body was full of sores. Lazarus wanted to eat the small pieces of bread that fell from the rich man's table. Even the dogs came and licked his sores.

"Then this poor man died, and the angels carried him away and put him at Abraham's side.

"The rich man also died and was buried. He was in hell and was suffering very much, and he looked up and saw Abraham far away, with Lazarus at his side.

"The rich man called out and said, 'Father Abraham, be merciful to me, and send Lazarus so he can put the end of his finger in water and make my tongue cool, because I am suffering in this fire.'

"But Abraham said, 'Son, remember you received your good things when you were alive, and

Lazarus received bad things. But Lazarus is comforted here now and you are suffering greatly. Also, there is a very large space that has been put between you and us, and no one can go from here to where you are and also no one can cross from there to come to us.'

"The rich man said, 'Father, then I ask you to send Lazarus to my father's house because I have five brothers, and he will warn them so they will not also come into this place to suffer.'

"But Abraham said, 'They have Moses and the prophets, so let them listen to them.'

"He said, 'No, Father Abraham, but they will repent if someone who was dead goes to them.'

"Abraham said to him, 'They will not be convinced if someone comes back to life from death, if they will not listen to Moses and the prophets.'"

Jesus went back across the Jordan to the place where John had baptized people at an earlier time, and He stayed there.

Many people came to Him, and they said, "It is true that John never did any miracles, but everything he said about this man was true."

Many people there believed in Him.

There was a sick man named Lazarus. He lived

in Bethany, the town where Mary and her sister, Martha, lived. This was the same Mary who anointed the Lord with perfume and dried his feet with her hair. It was her brother, Lazarus, who was sick.

So these sisters sent a message to Jesus and said, "Lord, the man whom You love is sick."

But when Jesus heard it, He said, "He will not die from this sickness. It is for the glory of God, so the Son of God can be given honor because of it."

Jesus loved Martha and her sister and Lazarus. But He stayed in the same place for two days after He heard that Lazarus was sick.

Then He said to His followers after this, "Let's go back to Judea."

His followers said to Him, "Teacher, the Jews tried to stone You, and You are going there again?"

He said to them, "Our friend Lazarus is sleeping, but I am going there so I can wake him."

His followers said to Him, "Lord, he will become well again, if he is sleeping."

Jesus was speaking about his death, but the followers thought He was speaking about regular sleep.

So Jesus said to them clearly, "Lazarus is dead, but I am happy for you that I was not there so you will believe. Let's go to Lazarus."

Then Thomas, who is also named Didymus, said to the other followers, "Let's also go so we can die with him."

When Jesus came, He found that Lazarus had been in the grave for four days already.

Bethany was about two miles away from Jerusalem, and many Jews had come to Martha and Mary to comfort them because of their brother.

Martha went out to meet Jesus when she heard He was coming, but Mary remained in the house.

Martha said to Jesus, "Lord, my brother would not have died if You had been here. But I know that even now God will give You anything You ask from Him."

Jesus said to her, "Your brother will come back to life again."

Martha said to Him, "I know he will come back to life again when people are brought back to life on the last day."

Jesus said to her, "I am the Resurrection and the Life. Any person who lives and believes in Me will never die. Do you believe this?"

She said to Him, "Yes, Lord, I believe You are the Christ, the Son of God, Who comes into the world."

After she said this, she went away and called her

sister Mary secretly and said, "The Teacher is here and He asks for you."

Mary got up quickly when she heard it and went to Him.

Jesus had not come into the town yet, but was still in the place where Martha met Him. The Jews who were comforting Mary in the house followed her when they saw her get up quickly and go out, because they thought she was going to the grave to cry there.

When Mary came to where Jesus was and saw Him, she fell at His feet.

She said to Him, "Lord, my brother would not have died if You had been here."

Jesus was deeply sad and troubled in His spirit when He saw that she and the Jews who came with her were crying.

He said, "Where did you put him?"

They said to Him, "Lord, come and see."

Jesus wept.

The Jews said, "See how much He loved Lazarus!"

But some of them said, "Couldn't this man who healed the eyes of people who were blind, stop Lazarus from dying?"

Jesus was deeply sad again, and He came to the

grave. It was a cave, and a stone was put across the front of it.

Jesus said, "Take away the stone."

Martha, the sister of the dead man said, "Lord, the body will have a bad smell now, because he has been dead for four days."

Jesus said to her, "Didn't I tell you that you would see the glory of God if you believe?"

So they took away the stone.

Jesus looked up and said, "Father, I thank You that You heard Me. I know You hear Me always. But I say this because of the people who stand near me, so they can believe that You sent Me."

After He said this, He called out with a loud voice, "Lazarus, come out!"

Then the man who was dead came out, and the graveclothes were tied around his hands and feet, and a cloth was around his face.

Jesus said to them, "Take off the graveclothes and let him go."

More than 700 years before this, the Jewish prophet Hosea foretold, **I will ransom them from the power of the graves; I will redeem them from death.**

Many of the Jews who came to Mary and saw what Jesus did believed in Him.

But some of them went away to the Pharisees and told them about the things Jesus did.

The chief priests and the Pharisees called the Jewish council to meet together, and they said, "What should we do? This Man is doing many miracles. All people will believe in Him if we let Him continue to do these things, and the Romans will come and take away our place and our nation."

But one of them, Caiaphas, who was the high priest that year, said to them, "You don't know anything. You don't know that it is better for you that one man dies for all the people and then all of the nation will not be lost."

He did not say this on his own. He was high priest that year, and because of this, he prophesied that Jesus would die for the nation, and that it was not for the nation only, but so He could also bring together the children of God, who are in many different places, into one group.

They made plans to kill Jesus from that day forward.

Jesus also told a story to some people who thought they were righteous and who thought other people were not as good as they were.

He said, "Two men went to the temple to pray.

One of the men was a Pharisee and the other one was a man to whom people paid taxes.

"The Pharisee stood and prayed this to himself, 'God, I thank You that I am not like the other men, who steal money from other people, or who are not fair to other people, or who are adulterers, or even who are like this man here to whom people pay taxes. I fast two times a week, and I give one-tenth from everything I have.'

"But the man to whom people paid taxes stood far away, and he would not even look up to heaven, but he hit his chest and said, 'God, be merciful to me. I am a sinner.'

"I say to you, this man returned to his house and was forgiven by God but the Pharisee was not forgiven.

"This is because everyone who tries to make himself important will be made humble and a person who makes himself humble will be made important."

People brought little children to Jesus so He could touch them. But His followers rebuked the people.

Jesus was very angry when He saw this, and said to them, "Let the little children come to me. Do not stop them, because the kingdom of God belongs to people who are like these little children. I tell you the truth, a person can never go into the kingdom of God if he does not accept the kingdom of God like a little child does."

He put His arms around them, and put His hands on them, and blessed them.

It was almost time for the Jewish Passover, and many people went from places outside the city to Jerusalem to make themselves pure.

They looked for Jesus there, and said to each other while they stood in the temple, "What do you think? Do you think He will not come to the feast?"

The chief priests and the Pharisees had ordered that any person should tell them if he knew where Jesus was, so they could take Him.

Jesus and His followers came near to Jerusalem, to Bethphage and Bethany, at the Mount of Olives.

Then Jesus sent two of His followers away, after He said to them, "Go into the next town that is ahead of you, and immediately you will find a young donkey tied there when you go into the town. No one has ever sat on this donkey. Untie it and bring it here. If anyone says to you, 'Why are you doing this?' say that the Lord needs it, and that He will return it soon."

They went and found a young donkey tied at a

door outside in the street, and they untied it.

Some people who stood there said to them, "Why are you untying the donkey?"

They told them what Jesus said, and the people allowed them to go.

They brought the young donkey to Jesus.

They put their coats on the road, and other people put down branches they cut from the fields.

The people who went ahead of Him and the people who followed Him shouted, "Hosanna, the One Who comes in the name of the Lord is blessed! The kingdom of our father David is coming and is blessed! Hosanna in the highest places!"

Long before, the prophet Zechariah had said, **Rejoice greatly, O daughter of Zion; shout, O daughter of Jerusalem: behold, thy King cometh unto thee: he is just, and having salvation; lowly, and riding upon a donkey ....**

All the people in Jerusalem were troubled when Jesus came into the city.

They asked, "Who is this?"

The people in the crowds said, "This is the prophet, Jesus, from Nazareth, in Galilee."

Jesus went into the temple of God, and He ordered all the people who bought and sold things in the temple to leave. He turned over the tables of the people who traded money, and He turned over the seats of the men who sold doves.

He said to them, "It is written, 'My house will be named a house of prayer,' but you have made it a place for thieves."

His followers remembered what was written in the scriptures, **"The zeal of thine house hath eaten me up."**

People who were blind and people who could not walk came to Him in the temple, and He healed them.

But the chief priests and the teachers of the Law were very angry when they saw the wonderful things He did and when they saw the children in the temple shouting, "Hosanna to the Son of David!"

They said to Him, "Do You hear what they are saying?"

Jesus said to them, "Yes, have you never read, 'You have made praise ready from the mouths of children and babies'?"

Jesus looked and saw the rich people put their gifts into the money box in the temple. He also saw a poor widow put in two small coins.

Jesus said, "I tell you the truth, this poor widow

put in more money than all these other people. This is because all of these people put in money that was part of their riches, but she is poor and she put in all the money she had."

Some of the people talked about the temple. It was made beautiful with the best stones and with gifts offered to God.

Jesus said, "The time will come when these things you see will not remain with one stone on top of another. Every one of them will be thrown down."

They asked Him, "Teacher, when will these things happen? What will be the sign to tell us when these things are ready to happen?"

He said, "Be careful that no one leads you in the wrong way, because many men will come using My name and say, 'I am He,' and, 'The time is near.' Do not go with them. Do not be afraid when you hear the sound of wars and trouble, because these things must happen first, but the end will not come yet."

Then He said to them, "Nations will come against other nations, and kingdoms come against other kingdoms, and there will be great earthquakes. In many places there will be diseases and there will not be any food. Things will happen that cause fear, and there will be great signs from heaven.

"There will be signs in the sun, moon, and stars, and the nations of the earth will be troubled because they will not understand the great sounds of the sea waves. Men will become weak because of fear and because of what is coming in the world, because the powers that are in the skies will be shaken.

"Then they will see the Son of Man come in a cloud with power and great glory. But look up and lift up your heads when these things begin to happen because your salvation will come soon.

"Be careful that your hearts and lives do not become filled by too much pleasure, by drinking, and by the worries of this life, because that day will come suddenly when you are not ready, and it will come to everyone who lives on the earth.

"But continue to be careful and pray so that you can be saved from all these things that will happen, and can be able to stand in the presence of the Son of Man."

Luke 16:19–31; John 10:40–11:8; John 11:11–16; John 11:17–44; Hosea 13:14; John 11:45–53; Luke 18:9–14; Mark 10:13–16; John 11:55–57; Mark 11:1–10; Zechariah 9:9; Matthew 21:10–13; John 2:17; Psalm 69:9; Matthew 21:14–16; Luke 21:1–11; Luke 21:25–28; Luke 21:34–36

CHAPTER 6

Then the chief priests and the religious leaders of the people came to the court of the high priest named Caiaphas. They talked to each other about how they could trick Jesus, take Him, and then kill Him.

But they said, "We should not do it during the feast, because the people could cause trouble and be violent if we do it then."

A woman who had an alabaster jar of expensive perfume came to Jesus when He was in Bethany, in Simon the leper's house. She poured it on His head while He was sitting at the table eating.

But His followers were angry when they saw it, and they said, "Why was this perfume wasted? It could be sold for a high price and the money could be given to the poor people."

But Jesus knew this and said to them, "Why do you trouble the woman? She has done a good thing to me. There will always be poor people with you, but I will not always be with you. She poured perfume on My body to make Me ready to be buried. I tell you the truth, what this woman has done will be spoken about in memory of her, wherever this gospel is preached in all the world."

Then one of the Twelve followers, named Judas Iscariot, went to the chief priests and said, "What will you give me if I give Jesus to you?"

They counted 30 pieces of silver money for him. After that time, Judas looked for the right time and place to betray Jesus to them.

The king and prophet David foretold this more than 1,000 years before, when he said, **Yea, mine own familiar friend, in whom I trusted, which did eat of my bread, hath lifted up his heel against me.**

Jesus' followers spoke with Him on the first day of the Feast of the Unleavened Bread, when they sacrificed the Passover lamb.

They said to Him, "Where do you want us to go to make things ready, so you can eat the Passover meal?"

He sent two of His followers after He said to them, "Go into the city, and you will meet a man there carrying a large jar of water. Follow him and say to the owner of the house he goes into, 'The Teacher asks, "Where is My guest room where I can eat the Passover meal with My followers?"' He will show you a large room upstairs with everything ready. Make things ready for us there."

His followers went out and came into the city. They found the things there just like He told them. Then they made the Passover meal ready.

Jesus came with the Twelve when it was evening.

He said to them as they lay down at the table and ate, "I tell you the truth, one of you who is eating with Me will betray Me."

They became deeply sad, and each one of the twelve asked Him, "It isn't I, is it?"

He said to them, "It is one of the Twelve. He is the man who puts bread into the same bowl with Me. The Son of man will die just like it was written about Him. But woe to that man through whom the Son of man will be betrayed. It would be better for that man if he had not been born."

Jesus took bread while they ate, and He thanked God for it. He broke it into pieces and gave it to His followers and said, "This is my body. Take it."

After He took a cup and thanked God for it, He gave it to them, and they all drank from it.

Then He said to them, "This is my blood that is poured out for many people. It represents the new agreement. I tell you the truth, I will not drink from the fruit of the vine again until that day when I drink it new in the Kingdom of God."

They went out to the Mountain of Olives after they sang a hymn.

Jesus said to them, "All of you will turn away from me because it is written, **'I will kill the shepherd, and the sheep will be spread out everywhere.'** But I will go into Galilee ahead of you after I am brought back to life from death."

But Peter said to Him, "I will not turn away from you even if everyone turns away."

Jesus said to him, "I tell you the truth, tonight you will say you do not know me three times, before the rooster crows two times."

But Peter continued to say even more strongly, "I will never say I do not know you, even if I must die with you!"

All the other followers said the same thing.

Jesus and the Twelve came to a place named Gethsemane, and He said to His followers, "Sit here while I pray."

He took Peter, James, and John with Him, and He was deeply sad and troubled.

Seven centuries before, Isaiah had foretold, **He is despised and rejected of men; a man of sorrows, and**

acquainted with grief.

Jesus said to them, "My soul is deeply sad. The sadness is almost killing Me. Stay here and watch."

He went a little farther, fell to the ground, and prayed for that time to leave Him if possible.

He said, "Abba, Father, it is possible for You to do all things. Take this cup away from Me. But let what You want happen, and not what I want."

Then He came to His followers and found them sleeping, and said to Peter, "Simon, are you sleeping? Couldn't you watch for one hour? Continue to watch and pray so you will not come into temptation. The spirit wants to do what is right, but the body is weak."

He went away again and prayed the same words.

Then He came again and found them sleeping, because their eyes were becoming tired. They did not know what to answer Him.

He came again the third time and said to them, "Are you still sleeping and resting? It is decided. The time has come. Look, the Son of Man will be betrayed soon to sinners. Get up. Let's go. The man who will betray me is here."

A crowd of people came as He spoke, and the man named Judas, who was one of the twelve, led the crowd. He came near Jesus to kiss Him.

But Jesus said to him, "Judas, will you betray the Son of Man with a kiss?"

When the men who were with Jesus saw what was going to happen, they said, "Lord, do You want us to fight with the sword?"

One of them hit the high priest's servant and cut off his right ear.

But Jesus answered, "Stop! No more of this!"

Then Jesus touched his ear and healed him.

Jesus said to the chief priests, the temple's officials, and the religious leaders who were against Him, "Have you come with swords and large sticks, like you take a thief? You did not try to take Me when I was in the temple with you every day. But this is your time, and the power of darkness rules."

They took Jesus, led Him away, and brought Him into the high priest's house.

But Peter walked far behind and followed Him.

They made a fire in the middle of the courtyard and sat together. Peter sat with them.

A servant girl saw him as he sat in the light of the fire, and she looked closely at him and said, "This man was also with Jesus."

But Peter said it was not true, and he said, "Woman, I do not know Him."

After a short time, another person saw him and said, "You are also one of their group."

But Peter said, "Man, I am not."

Another man said strongly about one hour later, "It is certain that this man also was with Jesus, because he is from Galilee."

But Peter said, "Man, I do not understand what you are saying!"

The rooster crowed as Peter spoke. The Lord turned and looked at Peter.

Then Peter remembered the words of the Lord and that He had said to him, "Before the rooster crows today, you will say three times that you do not know Me."

Peter went out and cried with deep sadness and shame.

The men who guarded Jesus laughed at Him and beat Him.

They covered His eyes and asked Him, saying, "Tell us by God's power, who is the person who hit You?"

They spoke many other evil things against Him.

The group of religious leaders of the people came together in the morning.

They were the chief priests and teachers of the

Law, and they led Him to their council and said, "Tell us if You are the Christ."

But He said to them, "You will not believe me if I tell you, and you will not answer if I ask you. But the Son of Man will be seated at the right hand of the power of God from this time forward."

All of them said, "Then are You the Son of God?"

He said to them, "You say that I am."

They said, "Why do we need any more reports when we have heard it from His own mouth?"

Then Judas, who betrayed Jesus, saw that He was condemned. Judas was deeply sorry, and he brought the pieces of silver money to the chief priests and religious leaders.

He said, "I have sinned, because I betrayed a man who was not guilty."

But they said, "We do not care about that. It is your problem."

He threw the pieces of silver money in the temple, went away, and hanged himself.

The chief priests took the pieces of silver money and said, "It is against the Law to put them into the money box, because it is the price paid for a man's blood."

So they decided to use the money to buy the potter's field to bury strangers in. That is why that field was named the Field of Blood, and that is still its name.

Then the things that Jeremiah the prophet spoke became true. He said, **"And they took the thirty pieces of silver, the price of him that was valued, and gave them for the potter's field, as the Lord appointed me."**

The religious leaders, teachers of the religious law, and all the council met together early in the morning.

They put chains on Jesus' arms and legs, led Him away, and gave Him to Pilate.

Pilate asked Him, "Are you the King of the Jews?"

Jesus answered him, "Yes, it is just as you have said it."

The chief priests said He was guilty of many things.

Pilate asked Jesus again, "Won't you answer any of these things? You heard the many things they say you are guilty of."

But Jesus did not answer anything, and Pilate was full of wonder.

The prophet Isaiah foretold this by the Holy Spirit more than 700 years before, when he said, **He was oppressed, and he was afflicted, yet he opened not his mouth; he is brought as a lamb to the slaughter, and** as a sheep before her shearers is dumb, so he openeth not his mouth.

Pilate usually freed a prisoner every year at the feast. He freed one prisoner the people asked for.

A man named Barabbas was in prison with the rebels who had killed other people in a rebellion.

The crowd of people went to Pilate and began to ask him to do for them what he usually did every year.

Pilate answered, "Do you want me to free the King of the Jews for you?"

Pilate said this because he knew the chief priests gave Jesus to him because they were jealous. But the chief priests convinced the crowd to ask Pilate to free Barabbas for them instead of Jesus.

Pilate answered again, "Then what should I do to the man whom you say is the King of the Jews?"

They shouted, "Kill Him on a cross!"

But Pilate said to them, "Why? What evil things has He done?"

But they shouted even louder, "Kill Him on a cross!"

Pilate wanted to please the crowd, so he freed Barabbas. He ordered them to beat Jesus, and he gave Him to them to hang Him on a cross to die.

The soldiers took Jesus away into the palace

named the Praetorium, and they called all the Roman soldiers to come there.

They dressed Him in purple clothes, and they made a crown of thorns and put it on His head.

They began to call out to Him, "Honor to the King of the Jews!"

Then they hit His head many times with a stick, spit at Him, and went down on their knees in front of Him.

Hundreds of years before, the prophet Isaiah had written about the Messiah, **I gave my back to the smiters, and my cheeks to them that plucked off the hair; I hid not my face from shame and spitting.**

They took the purple clothes off Him after they laughed at Him, and they put His own clothes on Him again.

Then they led Him out to hang Him on a cross to die.

Matthew 26:3–16; Psalm 41:9; Mark 14:12–31; Mark 14:32–33; Isaiah 53:3; Mark 14:34–42; Luke 22:47–62; Luke 22:63–71; Matthew 27:3–10; Mark 15:1–5; Isaiah 53:7; Mark 15:6–19; Isaiah 50:6; Mark 15:20

CHAPTER 7

There was a man from Cyrene, named Simon, who was the father of Alexander and Rufus. He walked near them as he came from outside the city, and they forced him to carry Jesus' cross.

They brought Jesus to the place named Golgotha. That means, 'The Place of the Skull.'

They offered Him wine mixed with myrrh, but He did not take it.

They hung Him on a cross and divided His clothes among them. They threw dice to decide what each person should take.

The king and prophet David foretold this incident more than 1,000 years before. He said, **They pierced my hands and my feet ... they look and stare upon me. They part my garments among them and cast lots upon my vesture.**

It was nine o'clock in the morning when they hung Him on a cross.

They wrote what they said He was guilty of: "The King of the Jews."

They also hung two thieves on crosses to die with Jesus. They put one thief at Jesus' right side and the other thief at His left side.

One of the men who did evil things and was also crucified, shamed Him and said, "Aren't You the Christ? Save yourself and save us."

But the other man rebuked him and said, "Don't you fear God, since you are given the same punishment? This punishment is what we deserve because of the evil things we did, but this Man has done nothing wrong."

He said, "Jesus, remember me when You come into Your kingdom."

Jesus said to him, "I tell you the truth, you will be with Me in Paradise today."

Isaiah prophesied about this more than 700 years before, **He hath poured out his soul until death; and he was numbered with the transgressors; and he bare the sin of many, and made intercession for the transgressors.**

Jesus' mother, her sister Mary, who was the wife of Clopas, and Mary Magdalene, were standing by His cross.

Jesus saw His mother and the follower whom He loved standing there, and He said to His mother,

"Woman, here is your son!"

He said to His follower, "Here is your mother!"

His follower took her into his home from that time forward.

The people who walked near Jesus shouted evil things against Him and shook their heads, saying, "Ha, You who were going to destroy the temple and build it again in three days, save yourself and come down from the cross!"

The chief priests and the teachers of the religious law laughed at Him with each other in the same way and said, "He saved other people, but He cannot save himself. The Christ, the King of Israel, should come down from the cross now so we can see it and believe in Him."

It became dark everywhere there at noon, and the darkness remained until three o'clock in the afternoon.

At that time, Jesus called out with a loud voice, "Eloi, Eloi, lama sabachthani?"

That means, "My God, My God, why have You turned away from Me?"

More than 1,000 years before, through King David, the Holy Spirit foretold that Jesus would say this, when David said those same words, **My God, My God, why** hast thou forsaken me?

Some people who stood near there heard it, and they said, "Listen, He is calling Elijah."

Then someone ran and filled a sponge with wine vinegar.

David also wrote about the Messiah, **And in my thirst they gave me vinegar to drink.**

The man put the sponge on a long stick, gave it to Jesus to drink, and said, "Leave Him alone now, and let us see if Elijah will come and take Him down from the cross."

The Holy Spirit spoke about this day through the Jewish prophet Isaiah more than 700 years before, **He is despised and rejected of men; a man of sorrows, and acquainted with grief, and we hid as if it were our faces from him; he was despised, and we esteemed him not. Surely he hath borne our griefs, and carried our sorrows; yet we did esteem him stricken, smitten of God, and afflicted. But he was wounded for our transgression, he was bruised for our iniquities; the chastisement of our peace was upon him, and with his stripes we are healed. All we like sheep have gone astray; we have turned every one to his own way, and the Lord hath laid on him the iniquity of us all.**

Jesus called out with a loud voice, and His life

left Him. Then the curtain in the temple was torn into two pieces. It tore from the top to the bottom.

When the chief officer who stood in front of Jesus saw the way He died, he said, "It is true that this Man was the Son of God."

It was Preparation Day, which is the day before the Sabbath, so Joseph from Arimathaea came when it was evening.

He was an important member of the Jewish Council who was also waiting for the Kingdom of God to come. He took courage and went to Pilate, asking him for the body of Jesus.

Joseph bought a very fine cloth, took Jesus down from the cross, and put the cloth around His body.

Then he put Jesus in a grave that was made by cutting a hole in rock, and he rolled a very large stone and put it against the door of the grave.

Mary Magdalene and Mary the mother of Joses saw where they put Jesus.

When the Sabbath day ended, Mary Magdalene, Mary the mother of James, and Salome bought spices so they could come and anoint His body.

They came to the grave very early on the first day of the week, after the sun came up.

They said to each other, "Who will roll away the stone from the door of the grave for us?"

They looked and saw that the stone was already rolled away, although it was a very large stone.

They went into the grave and saw a young man sitting at the right side of the grave. He was dressed in a white robe, and they were afraid.

He said to them, "Don't be afraid. You are looking for Jesus, the Nazarene, who died on a cross. He has been brought back to life! He is not here! Look, here is the place where they put Him! But go and tell His followers and Peter that He is going to Galilee ahead of you. You will see Him there just as He told you."

The women went out and ran away from the grave because they were full of fear and wonder and were shaking. They did not say anything to anyone, because they were afraid.

Jesus rose early on the first day of the week, and He appeared first to Mary Magdalene. She was the woman from whom He had ordered seven evil spirits to come out.

She went and told it to the people who had been with Him. They were deeply sad and crying.

They did not believe it when they heard He was

alive and that Mary had seen Him.

After that, Jesus came to two of His followers as they were walking out of the city into the country. But His appearance had changed.

Then they went away and told this to His other followers, but they did not believe those two followers either.

Jesus appeared to His followers again after this, at the sea of Tiberias. This was the way He appeared: Simon Peter, Thomas (also named Didymus), Nathanael from Cana in Galilee, the sons of Zebedee, and two of His other followers were together.

Simon Peter said to them, "I am going fishing."

They said to him, "We will also come with you."

They went out and got into the boat. They caught nothing that night.

Jesus stood on the shore when morning came, but His followers did not know it was Him.

Jesus said to them, "Children, do you have any fish?"

They answered Him, "No."

He said to them, "Throw your net on the right-hand side of the boat, and you will find some fish."

So they threw in the net, and then they were

unable to pull it in because of the large number of fish.

Then the follower whom Jesus loved said to Peter, "It is the Lord."

Simon Peter put on his coat when He heard it was the Lord (because he had taken it off). Then he jumped into the sea. But the other followers came in the boat, pulling the net full of fish. They were only about a hundred yards away from the land.

They saw a fire there when they came out on the land, and there were fish and some loaves of bread on it.

Jesus said to them, "Bring some of the fish you just caught."

So Simon Peter went up and pulled the net to the land. There were one hundred and fifty-three large fish in it. The net was not torn, although there were very many fish.

Jesus said to them, "Come and eat breakfast."

None of His followers had the courage to ask Him who He was, because they knew it was the Lord.

Jesus came and took the bread and gave it to them, and the fish also.

This was the third time Jesus appeared to His

followers after He was brought back to life from death.

The eleven followers went into Galilee, to the mountain where Jesus had told them to go.

They worshiped Him when they saw Him, but some of them had doubts.

Jesus came to them and spoke to them.

He said, "All authority has been given to me in heaven and on earth. So go to the people in all the nations, cause them to become My followers, and baptize them in the name of the Father, the Son, and the Holy Spirit. Teach them to obey everything that I have commanded you. I will be with you always, even until the end of the world."

Then the Lord Jesus was taken up into heaven after He spoke to them, and He sat at the right side of God.

They looked up to heaven as Jesus went, and two men in white clothes stood beside them.

They said, "You men of Galilee, why do you stand here looking up to heaven? This Jesus, who was taken up to heaven from you, will come again in the same way that you saw Him go into heaven."

His followers went out and preached everywhere. The Lord worked with them and proved His message was true because of the signs that followed the message.

❧

And so, the words of the angel to Mary were fulfilled, Mary, don't be afraid, because you are favored by God. You will conceive in your body and give birth to a son, and you will name Him Jesus. He will be great and will be called the Son of the Most High God. The Lord God will give Him the throne of His father David. He will rule over the house of Jacob forever, and His kingdom will never end.

And the words of the angel to Joseph were fulfilled, Joseph, you who are from the family of David, do not be afraid to take Mary to be your wife, because the baby who is inside her is from the Holy Spirit. She will give birth to a son, and you will name Him 'Jesus', because He will save His people from their sins.

And the words of the angel to the shepherds were fulfilled, Do not be afraid, because I bring you good news about great joy for all people. Your Savior was born today in the city of David. He is Christ the Lord.

And the words of Jesus to us are fulfilled, I tell you

the truth, whoever hears My message and believes the One who sent Me, has everlasting life. He will not be condemned, but he has gone from death into life.

Mark 15:21-24; Psalm 22:16-18; Mark 15:25-27;
Luke 23:39-43; Isaiah 53:12; John 19:25-27; Mark 15:29-34;
Psalm 22:1; Mark 15:35,36; Psalm 69:21; Mark 15:36;
Isaiah 53:3-6; Mark 15:37-38; Mark 15:39; Mark 15:42-43;
Mark 15:46-47; Mark 16:1-7; Mark 16:8-13; John 21:1-14;
Matthew 28:16-20; Mark 16:19; Acts 1:10-11; Mark 16:20;
Luke 1:30-33; Matthew 1:20-21; Luke 2:10-11; John 5:24

ℒIFE'S GREATEST DECISION

𝒯wo great moments in our lives are when we are born and when we discover why we were born. We were created for a reason—a divine purpose. Our lives are not accidents or fate. God has a personal plan for each of us. His purpose in our lives can only be accomplished because of Jesus Christ.

The apostle Peter was a fisherman who traveled with Jesus for more than three years, listening to His teaching and observing His life. Peter was one of Jesus' first followers and became one of His closest friends. In a letter Peter wrote late in his life, he said, "We did not follow cleverly invented stories when we told you about the power and coming of our Lord Jesus Christ, but we were eyewitnesses of his majesty."[1]

The Book of Acts in the New Testament, records a simple and clear presentation Peter gave about Jesus Christ to a Roman named Cornelius:

> "I now realize how true it is that God does not show favoritism but accepts men from every

nation who fear him and do what is right. You know the message God sent to the people of Israel, telling the good news of peace through Jesus Christ, who is Lord of all. You know what has happened throughout Judea, beginning in Galilee after the baptism that John preached— how God anointed Jesus of Nazareth with the Holy Spirit and power, and how he went around doing good and healing all who were under the power of the devil, because God was with him. We are witnesses of everything he did in the country of the Jews and in Jerusalem. They killed him by hanging him on a tree, but God raised him from the dead on the third day and caused him to be seen. He was not seen by all the people, but by witnesses whom God had already chosen—by us who ate and drank with him after he rose from the dead. He commanded us to preach to the people and to testify that he is the one whom God appointed as judge of the living and the dead. All the prophets testify about him that everyone who believes in him receives forgiveness of sins through his name."[2]

The life of Christ calls for a decision. Was He just a great teacher and spiritual leader? Or was He who He claimed to be—the Son of God who has the power to forgive sin and grant everlasting life to all who will believe on Him?

The proofs that Christ came back to life from death were so convincing the early Christians gave their lives rather than deny that Jesus was the Son of God.

Jesus Christ taught that every person will exist for eternity. Life has only two roads, and we are each on one of them. One leads to death and eternal punishment—the other to everlasting life. The apostle Paul wrote to the Roman Christians: "For the wages of sin is death, but the gift of God is eternal life in Christ Jesus our Lord."[3] He also taught that being saved from sin's penalty is simple: "If you confess with your mouth, 'Jesus is Lord,' and believe in your heart that God raised him from the dead, you will be saved."[4]

We all know in our hearts that we have sinned. Even if we have never read a Bible or do not understand what it means to sin against God, we can know we are sinners, because God created each of us with a conscience. We know what we don't want others to do to us. We don't want them to steal our possessions, lie about us or be unkind to us. When we do to someone what we don't want done to us, our conscience lets us know we have done wrong.

The penalty for sin is death. That is why all people die. But 2,000 years ago, Jesus Christ, the holy Son of God, became a man. For 33 years He lived without sin. Then He was killed. He paid the penalty for sin without committing the crime. So death had no power over Him. After three days, He came back to life again. He is alive! And now He offers forgiveness of sin and the gift of everlasting life to everyone who will ask Him.

You can receive Christ as your Savior right now, this moment! You don't have to be in a church or special place, or have the help of a minister or priest.

You can pray now, wherever you are. God is listening. Tell Him in your own words that you are sorry for your sins and that you want to receive Jesus Christ as your Savior and Lord. Ask God to help you change your heart and life. It's your prayer He wants to hear. You can pray the following prayer, but it is not enough just to say the words. You must mean it from your heart:

"God, I believe you have a purpose and plan for my life. But, I know I have sinned. I believe Your Son, Jesus Christ, died to take the punishment for my sin. I believe Jesus came back to life from death and has the power to forgive my sin and change my life. Forgive me. Come into my life and change me. I want to live for You and follow Your plan for my life, in Jesus' name."

God has forgiven you if you prayed this prayer and meant it from your heart. God knew before you were born that you would receive His Son as your Savior. Now you can begin the life He has planned for you! Step by step God will lead you to what He has chosen for you. He will show you the way to live and will teach you each day as you grow spiritually and become the person He planned for you to be.

Your commitment to Christ is not just religion, it is a relationship. There are four basic things that will greatly help you in your relationship with Jesus and help you to grow spiritually.

1) *You need spiritual food.* You know that if you don't eat for a few days your body gets weak. You are not just a body. Your spirit needs food like your body does or you will become spiritually weak. The Bible is God's Word. It is like spiritual food. We suggest you start by spending just five or ten minutes each day reading the Bible. You can start with the Gospel of Mark, which is the earliest and shortest record of the life of Jesus.

2) *You need to pray each day.* In any personal relationship, we need to talk to each other. When you

read your Bible each day, spend time talking to God. Just speak to Him in your own words from your heart. Also spend a few moments just quietly thinking about what you've read in the Bible. God will communicate to your heart and guide you.

3) *You need a spiritual family.* That's what a church is. We can't make it in life alone. Your church family will help you grow stronger in Christ. They will be there to encourage you, be your friends, and pray with you. So, find a church home and be there every Sunday. Attend a church where Christ is honored, the Bible is taught, and everyone is welcome.

4) *You need to tell others.* When something wonderful happens, you want to tell other people about it! You will continue to find that the new life Jesus Christ has given you is the greatest thing that has ever happened to you. You know already that God has a plan for your life. A great part of that plan is that God will use you to tell others about the new life they can have in Christ. There are people only you can reach with the Good News about Jesus!

Jesus commanded us to tell others what He has done for us and what He will do for them. Some will receive that message and others will not. But we must obey Jesus and tell the good news so everyone has the opportunity to receive forgiveness of sin and the gift of everlasting life.

Before you were born, God had a plan and purpose for your life. Receiving Christ has opened the way for that plan for you.

The followers of Christ who prepared and distributed this book pray that God will continue to bless you and make you a blessing to others.

[1]2 Peter 1:16
[2]Acts 10:34-43
[3]Romans 6:23
[4]Romans 10:9,10

The above Scriptures are taken from the New International Version of the Bible.